Joe Biden

by Alex Monroe

BELLWETHER MEDIA • MINNEAPOLIS, MN

BLASTOFF! READERS

2

Blastoff! Readers are carefully developed by literacy experts to build reading stamina and move students toward fluency by combining standards-based content with developmentally appropriate text.

Level 1 provides the most support through repetition of high-frequency words, light text, predictable sentence patterns, and strong visual support.

Level 2 offers early readers a bit more challenge through varied sentences, increased text load, and text-supportive special features.

Level 3 advances early-fluent readers toward fluency through increased text load, less reliance on photos, advancing concepts, longer sentences, and more complex special features.

★ **Blastoff! Universe**

Reading Level

Grade **K**

Grades **1–3**

Grade **4**

This edition first published in 2022 by Bellwether Media, Inc.

No part of this publication may be reproduced in whole or in part without written permission of the publisher. For information regarding permission, write to Bellwether Media, Inc., Attention: Permissions Department, 6012 Blue Circle Drive, Minnetonka, MN 55343.

Library of Congress Cataloging-in-Publication Data

Names: Monroe, Alex (Writer of children's books), author.
Title: Joe Biden / by Alex Monroe.
Description: Minneapolis, MN : Bellwether Media, Inc., 2022. | Series: Blastoff! Readers: American Presidents | Includes bibliographical references and index. | Audience: Ages 5-8 | Audience: Grades 2-3 | Summary: "Relevant images match informative text in this introduction to Joe Biden. Intended for students in kindergarten through third grade"-- Provided by publisher.
Identifiers: LCCN 2021011403 (print) | LCCN 2021011404 (ebook) | ISBN 9781644875162 (library binding) | ISBN 9781648344848 (paperback) | ISBN 9781648344244 (ebook)
Subjects: LCSH: Biden, Joseph R., Jr.--Juvenile literature. | Presidents--United States--Biography--Juvenile literature. | United States--Politics and government--2021---Juvenile literature.
Classification: LCC E917 .M66 2022 (print) | LCC E917 (ebook) | DDC 973.934092 [B]--dc23
LC record available at https://lccn.loc.gov/2021011403
LC ebook record available at https://lccn.loc.gov/2021011404

Editor: Elizabeth Neuenfeldt   Designer: Josh Brink

Printed in the United States of America, North Mankato, MN.

Table of Contents

Joe Biden is the 46th president of the United States. He was **elected** in 2020.

4

More people voted for him
than any other president!

WWW.JOEBIDEN.COM

BID=N

=SIDENT

Joe was born in 1942. He first lived in Pennsylvania.

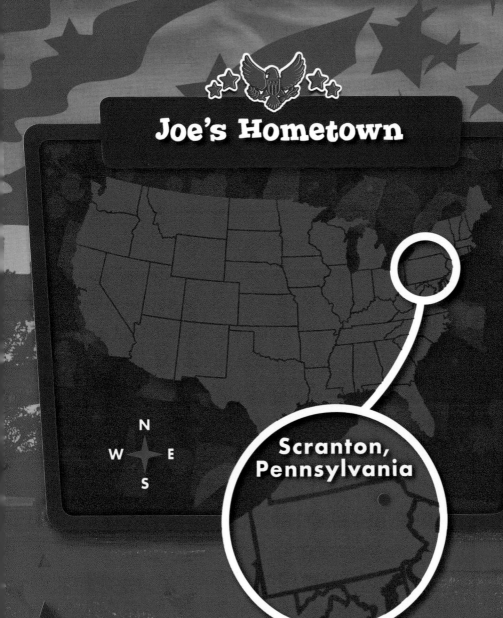

Joe's Hometown

N
W • E
S

Scranton,
Pennsylvania

He was **bullied** for his **stutter**.
He read poetry to help his speech.

Joe's family later
moved to Delaware.

Presidential Picks

Pets

two German shepherd
dogs, Champ and Major

Foods

pasta and chocolate
chip ice cream

Movie

Chariots of Fire

Sports

baseball and football

Joe at
Archmere Academy

Joe studied hard. He got into a good high school. He worked to help pay for it.

Joe studied **political science** in college. He studied history, too.

Syracuse University
College of Law

Then, he went to New York.
He attended law school.

Afterwards, Joe returned to Delaware. In 1973, he became a **senator**. He served for 36 years!

He worked with other countries. He passed laws for **gender equality**.

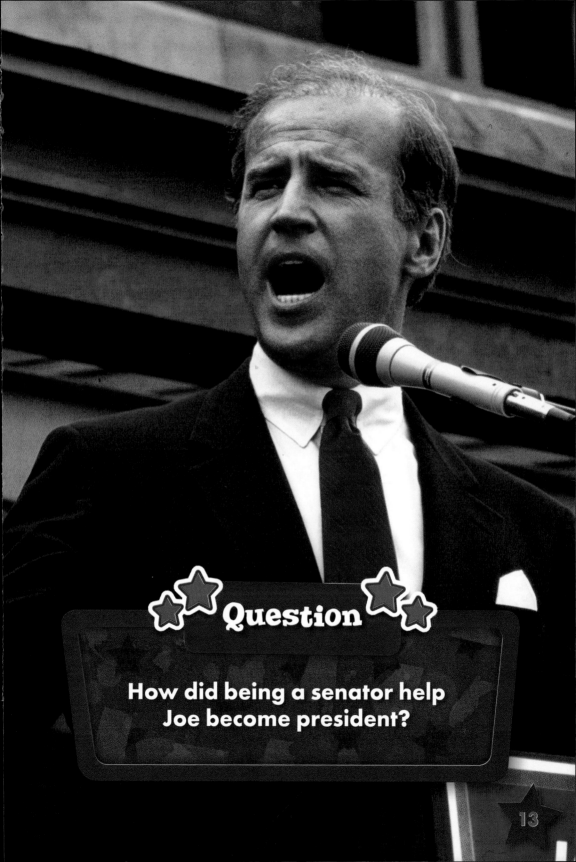

Question

How did being a senator help
Joe become president?

13

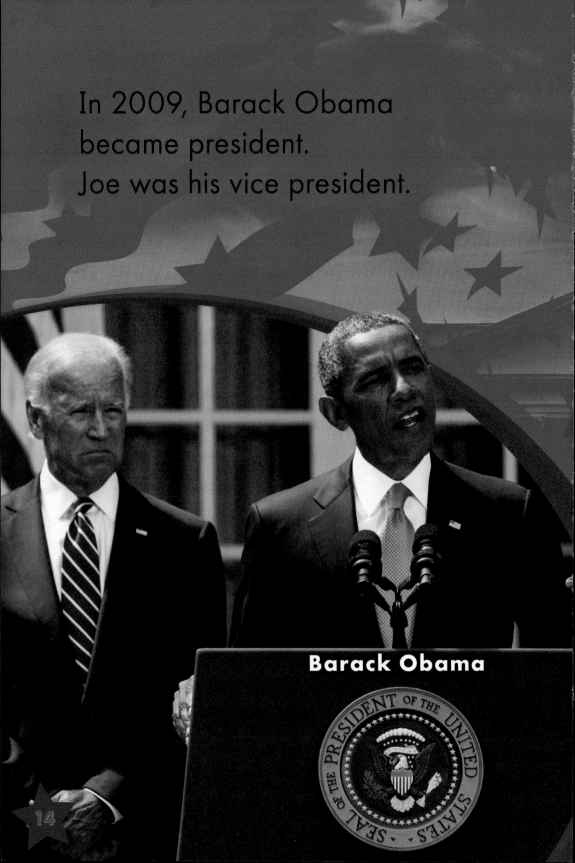

In 2009, Barack Obama became president.
Joe was his vice president.

Barack Obama

14

They helped the **economy** grow. They helped people get health care, too.

Time In Office

In 2020, Joe ran for president. He won!

Joe took office in 2021.
He quickly got to work.

Presidential Profile

Place of Birth

Scranton, Pennsylvania

Birthday

November 20, 1942

Schooling

University of Delaware
and Syracuse University

Term

started in 2021

Party

Democratic

Signature

Vice President

Kamala
Harris

17

Joe signing
orders

The **coronavirus pandemic** harmed many people. Joe signed orders to help. Joe took steps to fight **climate change**. He made plans to help **immigrants**.

Joe Timeline

November 7, 2020

Joe Biden is
elected president

January 20, 2021

Joe takes office

January 20, 2021

Joe rejoins the Paris
Agreement to fight
climate change

January 21, 2021

Joe signs 10 orders to
help fight coronavirus

February 18, 2021

Joe introduces a path
for immigrants to
become citizens

19

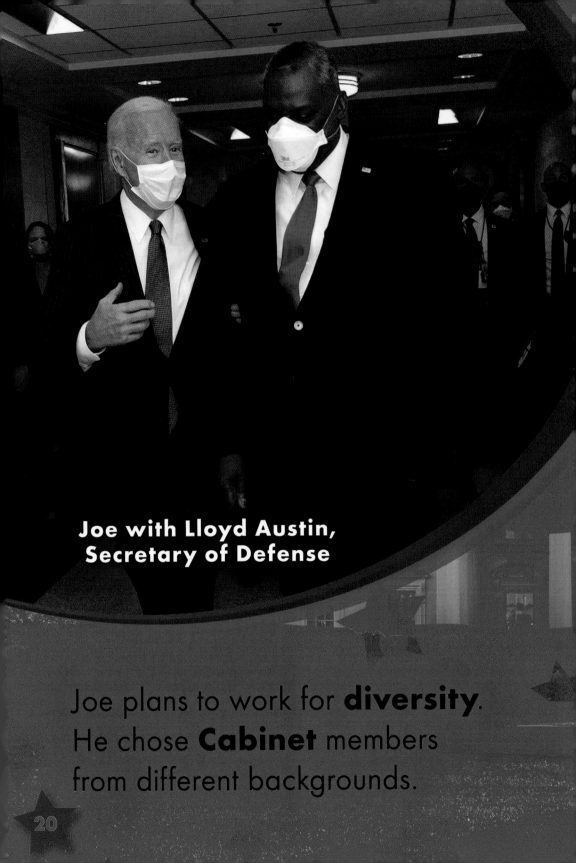

Joe with Lloyd Austin,
Secretary of Defense

Joe plans to work for **diversity**.
He chose **Cabinet** members
from different backgrounds.

His presidency gives
hope to many people!

21

Glossary

bullied—to be scared or harmed by others

Cabinet—a group of people who give advice to the leader of a government

climate change—a human-caused change in Earth's weather due to warming temperatures

coronavirus pandemic—an outbreak of the COVID-19 virus starting in December 2019 that led to millions of deaths and shutdowns around the world

diversity—the inclusion of people of different races, genders, and backgrounds in a group

economy—the way a state or country makes, sells, and uses goods and services

elected—chosen by voting

gender equality—the state in which all genders have equal rights and opportunities

immigrants—people who move to a new country

political science—the study of systems of government

senator—a member of the Senate of the U.S. government; the Senate helps make laws.

stutter—a type of speech in which the speaker repeats speech sounds without meaning to or has difficulty making speech sounds

To Learn More

AT THE LIBRARY

Anderson, Kirsten. *Who Is Kamala Harris?* New York, N.Y.: Penguin Workshop, 2021.

Hansen, Grace. *Joe Biden*. Minneapolis, Minn.: Abdo Kids, 2021.

McCullough, Joy. *Champ and Major: First Dogs*. New York, N.Y.: Dial Books, 2021.

ON THE WEB

FACTSURFER

Factsurfer.com gives you a safe, fun way to find more information.

1. Go to www.factsurfer.com.

2. Enter "Joe Biden" into the search box and click 🔍.

3. Select your book cover to see a list of related content.

Index

The images in this book are reproduced through the courtesy of: White house photo by David Lienemann/ Wikimedia Commons, cover; Geopix/ Alamy, p. 3; Don Mennig/ Alamy, p. 4; Stratos Brilakis, p. 5; ARCHIVIO GBB/ Alamy, p. 7; The White House/ Wikimedia Commons, p. 8 (dogs); Anna Shepulova, p. 8 (pasta); A.F. ARCHIVE/ Alamy, p. 8 (Chariots of Fire); Artur Didyk, p. 8 (baseball); Office of the United States Senator Joe Biden (D - Delaware)/ Wikimedia Commons, p. 9; University of Delaware/ Wikimedia Commons, p. 10; debra millet/ Alamy, p. 11; Bettmann/ Contributor/ Getty Images, p. 12; Cynthia Johnson/ Contributor/ Getty Images, p. 13; dpa picture alliance/ Alamy, pp. 14, 18; Jim West/ Alamy, p.15; American Photo Archive/ Alamy, pp. 16, 19 (immigration); Joe Biden/ Wikimedia Commons, p. 17 (signature); Nuno21, p. 17; archna nautiyal, p. 19 (Joe takes office); JOHNATHAN ERNST/ Alamy, p. 19 (Coronavirus orders); DOD Photo/ Alamy, p. 20; Drew Angerer/ Staff/ Getty Images, p. 21; Christopher Sciacca, p. 23.